Joseph Grinnell Dalton

Lyra Bicyclica

Forty Poets on the Wheel

Joseph Grinnell Dalton

Lyra Bicyclica
Forty Poets on the Wheel

ISBN/EAN: 9783337777753

Printed in Europe, USA, Canada, Australia, Japan

Cover: Foto ©Thomas Meinert / pixelio.de

More available books at **www.hansebooks.com**

Lyra Bicyclica:

FORTY POETS ON THE WHEEL.

BY

J. G. DALTON.

ERIPUIT MUSÆ IGNEM, CARMENQUE CANENTI.

BOSTON:
PUBLISHED FOR THE AUTHOR.
1880.

Bicyclian bards who sung
   Wheely ideas below,
Which always find us young,
   Or always make us so.

PREFATORY.

THE unprecedented peculiarities of most of the verses herein contained seem to be warrant enough for their collection into a volume. Doubtless a new *Ars poetica*, with a wholly novel subject (though narrow), should float a book, if it be not otherwise insufferably heavy.

The author-compiler is one of the very first Bostonians who, in the latter part of the year 1877, began to ride and write into notice the bicycle in this country. A few words also seem needful here in explanation of his entering upon the manufacture of this "machine poetry,"— such in a fuller sense of the term than it ever had before.

Under the early exhilarating effect of the wiry transit, in a sportive communication to a city paper (the *Globe* of Jan. 9, '78) he called upon our native poets, naming some in particular, to favor us with a song or two for the new move, declaring that its peculiar charms and potencies deserved and awaited an adequate celebration. Strange to say, no response to this invitation was forthcoming, excepting a brief trifle signed O. W. H. (now on p. 20 of this volume) in the same paper a short time after. Thanks for small favors; but, in the opinion of the present writer, sustained bursts of panegyrical song were needed to meet the demands of the occasion! How to get them? Having little confidence in his own capacity for poetry, he sought aid through the old proverb about "birds that can sing and won't sing," and soon hit upon the surprising discovery that the meaning of poems can be extracted, and a new one substituted, without injuring the form. So the Chinese will vacuate an egg or an orange of its original contents, fill it with strange confections, and leave no discernible break. In our case the diligent artificer sometimes sees opportunities of improving the exterior also. From trying this process upon the two distinguished poets who had neglected his modest request, the writer has developed the Bi-lyrical Method, and extended his scheme of confiscation over the whole domain of available song. — "Insatiate Bicycler, would not two suffice?" says the gentle reader. Not a bit of it: refused a little, he will ravage much. There are, however, quite a number of pieces radically his own, which the proficient reader will easily distinguish. Nearly all have appeared in papers of this city, or in England, and are now revised and improved.

Mindful of the fate of Marsyas, and that of the dilated frog in the fable, he presents them to the reading public, who should kindly make due allowance for the spirit of youth and the Wheel; and he dedicates them to the gathering army of bicyclers on this continent, with the motto, —

Rota non furor brebis est.

CONTENTS.

	PAGE
PREFATORY	1
PRELUSIONS FROM THE POETS	9
THE HARP OF ROTA	11
THE OVER-CYCLES	12
INITIAL AND CELESTIAL CYCLING	14
THE TREAD-WHEEL SONG	19
THE YOUTH AND THE BICYCLE	20
A TOAST	21
MY BICYCLE	22
TRANSLATIONS VERY MUCH TRANSLATED FROM LONGFELLOW:—	
THE CELESTIAL CYCLER	25
SONG OF THE SILENT WHEEL	27
THE CYCLE ON THE ROAD	29
THE EARTH HATH ITS GEMS	30
THE WHEEL	31
PEGASUS IN (ABOUT 40) POUND	32
THE LADDER OF ST. HYGEIA	34
THE STILLY WHEEL	36
BICYCLICALISTHENICS	39
YANKEE-LAND	40

CONTENTS.

	PAGE
LAY OF THE PEDESTRIAN	42
THE BICYCLE	43
HASTE NOT, PAUSE NOT	44
THE STEED OF FIRE	45
BISAKEL	47
GRAND CHORUS	49
OWED TO THE BICYCLE	50
THOSE BICYCLES	51
ANACREON: ODE XXXIX.	52
ROTAL POESY	53
FROM THE GREEK	54
THE DANDY BICYCLER	55
LITTLE MISS LOQUITUR	56
"MUSIC" ON THE WIRE	56
ROTA ANGLICA	58
THE WHEEL-SHOP	58
CARMEN BICYCLICUM	59
FLEET WHEEL	61
WHAT TO DO	61
HIS FIRST RIDE	62
"MORTALITY" ENLIVENED	63
SONG TO BISAKEL	65
WHERE'S MY JOHN?	66
CAREFUL SENIOR'S SONG	68
THE PILGRIM	71
THE LIGHT OF THE STUD	71
THE WHEELLESS	72
A HYMNLET	73

CONTENTS.

	PAGE
SOLILOQUY OF A WARY WOBBLER	74
THE PHANTOM OF DELIGHT	74
IN RUNNING'EM & CO.'S SALESROOM	76
HYGEIA'S WHEEL	77
A MERRY CAR	79
ELDERS, COME UP	81
TO MIDDEL AGER, ESQ.	82
WINTRY MUSINGS	82
ADAPTED ODE	84
"MY LOVE," A SPOOPSY POEM	85
A HEADER	86
ROTA FELIX	87
"GONDOLA" MADE BICYCLE	87
RHYMES OF THE ROAD	88
SONNETS BY WHEELIAM SHAKESPOKE:—	
TO ABEL ELDER	90
THE REASONS WHY	91
TO BISAKEL	93
THE BICYCLER; A VAGARY	95
CAMPBELL UNDONE AND OUTDONE	96
ALTA CANENS	97
APOLOGY	98
NON ASSUMPSIT	99
WHEELY THOUGHTS AND EJACULATIONS:—	
ROTALIS EQUITATUS	100
ARE YOU READY?	101
SLICK TRANSIT GLORIA BICYCLI	102
POEM OF THE RIDE	104

PRELUSIONS FROM THE POETS.

In seipso totus teres atque rotundus.
HORACE.

And wondrous was his way, and wondrous was his coach.
COWLEY.

> Mighty stage of mortal scenes,
> Drest with strong and gay machines.
WATTS.

Since the time of horse-consuls, now long out of date,
No nags ever made such a stir in the state.
MOORE.

What wondrous new machines have late been spinning!
BYRON.

> I have been
> On friendly terms with this machine.
WORDSWORTH.

> Sublime on radiant wires he rode,
> To draw a fame so truly circular.
DRYDEN.

Now proceed,
And sing the extension of the iron horse
Made by John Taurus with Minerva's aid,
And by the safe Cunarder carefully
Conveyed unto the Bay State capital,
Where charméd starters of its boom did take
The city taste. And I, if thou relate
The story rightly, will to all declare
That largely hath the bounteous god of ride
Bestowed on thee the wheely shift of song.

[From a new Odyssey, B. viii.: Ulysses to the minstrel sage, Demodocus, of the " clear-toned harp."]

LYRA BICYCLICA.

THE HARP OF ROTA.

MORE of a strain than merely my
    Verse sounds the iron wheel along:
Caught on the wings of wire to fly
    Above the pitch of single song,

Poe, Moore, and Byron tuneful climb,
    Emerson's native graces play,
With ring of Whitman's chanting chime
    And gentle Longman's moral lay.

William the Great me visited!
    Drawn to the glimpses of the wheel;
Cæsar nor Phœbus had, he said,
    Car fashioned so, "in cómplete steel."

Full many more were coaxed to aid ;
And thus a middling pen, or worse,
On lines of classic models made
Diverted and diverting verse.

Some bicycles long since had birth
Ere Coventry so many named
And raised new ridings o'er the earth
On those gay rollers greatly framed.

Vain was the brief boneshakers' ride,
They had no go-it, and they died.
In vain they seemed, inane they fled ;
They made no poet, and are dead.

———•———

THE OVER-CYCLES.

BY R. W. E. + D.

Lo ! New England answers Old.
Walker, break this sloth urbane ;
A Wheeling voice bids be uprolled
Misty gray dreams which thee detain.

THE OVER-CYCLES.

Mark how the climbing cycle-boys
Beckon thee to all their joys,
Horsed on a tipsy hoop of steel —
Pedepulsion on a wheel.
Youth, by a "mount" make free thy way,
Teach thy feet to feel the pedal,
Ere yet arrives the wintry day
Time with thy feet shall meddle.
Accept the bounty of the high cycle,
Taste the lordship of the bicycle.

Oh, what is the cause metaphysical
Past ages have scarce met a bicycle —
    That Menu and Plato,
    And Plutarch and Cato,
Should have seldom bestridden the bicycle?
The Sphinx don't know nothing about 'em;
Monadnoc inclineth to doubt 'em;
Bold Cæsar went onward without 'em;
    But how Eze-kiēl
    Often plieth "the wheel"!
Have the prophets best ridden the bicycle?

INITIAL AND CELESTIAL CYCLING.

A PARODY-MOSAIC.

I.

BICYCLIC knights I often spy,
On horse uncarnate riding by;
Nimbly they scale his vaulty back,
And spin along the travelled track.
I see men go up and down,
In the country and the town,
Who on two wheels throned sedate
Have not hazarded their state:
With speedful limbs and agile toes
Lusty Juventus circling goes,
And Oldster's legs, aware of wane,
Revivify and dance again.
They are there for benefit;
They are there from drudging quit,
And Wisdom journeying on the road
Daily stops to view their mode.

On pedalian pinions fleeting,
See them twirl the witching wheel,

INITIAL AND CELESTIAL CYCLING.

Orb-libration's magic beating
In the tense and vibrant steel.
My soul the mystic carol sings
Of those silent circling wings :
It is ever the self-same tale,
The first experience will not fail;
Only two in the garden walked,
And with snake and seraph talked :
Cycles only two are twirled,
Yet how steadfastly they run,
To the cadence of the whirling world
That dances round the sun.
Unheeded Danger near him strides,
He laughs that on bicycle rides.

I bend my fancy to their leading,
All too nimble for my treading;
My metric feet are no account
To lift me to their wheely mount,
And much revolving in my mind
Turns up no chance of seat behind.
Keen my sense, my heart was young,
Right good-will my sinews strung,
But no speed of mine avails
To hunt upon their narrow trails;

Fleetest couriers alive,
Never yet could I arrive.
Sometimes their strong speed they slacken,
Though they are not overtaken;
On and away, their hasting feet
Make the morning proud and sweet:
Bright on the cheeks of gay and staid
The rose of action burns;
Though breeches wear, and coats may fade,
Immortal youth returns.

II.

The soul regards with equal ken
The dancing Pleiads and our frolic men.
Bird, that from the nadir's floor
To the zenith top can soar,
Light rides the arch of night and noon,
Bicycling on the sun and moon;
So orbit of the muse exceeds
All such as now we erring own,
Which seeming firm mechanic steeds,
Are shadows flitting up and down.
Spirit that lurks such form within
Beckons to spirit in the skin;

INITIAL AND CELESTIAL CYCLING.

Self-kindled every semblance glows,
And hints the future which it owes.
Hear you then, bicycle fellows,
Fits not to be over-zealous;
Steeds not to work on the clean jump,
Nor wind nor heart perpetual pump.

    Profounder and higher
    Man's spirit must strive;
    To his aye-rolling orbit
    No goal will arrive;
    The cycles that now draw him
    With fleetness untold,
    Once known, — for new cycles
    He spurneth the old.

    Deep lore lieth under
    These circlets of time;
    They melt in the light of
    Their meaning sublime.
    Love works at the axle,
    Beholdeth the way;
    Forth speed the strong pulses
    To the borders of day.

Loftier rounds, a purer air,
Ye shall climb on the heavenly stair;
Your reach shall yet be more profound,
And a vista without bound;
The axis of the wheels you steer
Be the axis of the sphere,
And the lustre and the grace
Which fascinate each youthful heart,
Beam from cosmic counterpart
Translucent through immortal face,
Where they that swiftly come and go
Leave no track on the heavenly snow.

Upward, higher far,
Over sun and star,
Thou must learn to mount,
Into vision where all form
In one only form dissolves;
In a region where the wheel
On which all beings ride
Visibly revolves;
Where the starred eternal worm
Girds the world with bound and term.

THE TREAD-WHEEL SONG.

ADAPTED FROM HOLMES.

THE stars are rolling in the sky,
    The earth rolls on below,
And we can feel our twinkling wheel
    Revolving as we go.
Then tread away, my gallant boys,
    And make the axle fly;
Why should not we go rotiform,
    Like planets in the sky?

Wake up, come up, you walking men,
    And stir your heavy pegs;
Arouse, arise, my gawky friend,
    And ply your spider legs!
What tho' you're awkward at the first,
    'Most any one can learn —
So hold upon the handles, man,
    And take another turn.

They've built us up a noble steed
    To beat the vulgar rout;

The motion is almost the same
   As just to walk about.
You 're seated on horseback afoot,
   To speed your distant ends;
Beside the pleasant rolling round
   Among one's honest friends.

Mark, fellows, 't is a Traveller,
   And useful work is done,
As well as on its spinning wings
   To fly around for fun.
You 'll say, when our revolving colt
   You shall have better known,
"Now, hang me, but I must have one
   Bicycle of my own!"

THE YOUTH AND THE BICYCLE.

A CERTAIN young man, for his physical,
Has been out and bought him a bicycle;
   He is careless and rash,
   And it 's treating him "hash,"
This hasty young man on his bicycle.

Says he, you acephalous bicycle,
I shall fling you away for a tricycle,
   Have a *tertium quid*,
   Or it cannot be rid,
Says hasty young man off his bicycle.

O. W. H.

A TOAST.

HOLMES PLUS D.

BIBAMUS AD PRIMUM BICYCLICUM CLUB,
IN URBE EORUM CUI NOMEN EST "HUB";
ET FLOREANT, VALEANT, VOLITANT TAM,
NON PEIRCIUS IPSE ENUMERET QUAM.

Englished, freely.

HERE's luck to the pioneer Bicycle Club,
That starts in the place entitled the Hub;
May their growth, example, and circling be such,
Not Peirce's own chalk can reckon how much.

MY BICYCLE.

BY JAGY TORLTON.

He cadgily ranted and sang. — Old Song.

WHAT spins around "like all git out,"
And swiftly carries me about, —
So light, so still, so bright and stout?
                      My Bicycle.

Regard me now where I sit high on
Nag forty pound of mostly iron;
And don't you wish that you might try on
                      My Bicycle?

Monstrum informe, ingens! some
Cry, seeing first this courser come.
Our "fine knee-action" strikes them dumb,
                      My Bicycle!

Calling him monster from the east,
And both a lean and fatuous beast,
You comprehend not in the least
                      My Bicycle.

MY BICYCLE.

Revolve it in your mind, and my way
Will show to be a more than *guy* way —
High way of riding on the highway —
My Bicycle.

Those now who stand and stare and say,
O, "*parce nobis, s'il vous plait,*"
Will beg to tread, another day,
My Bicycle.

What tho' Hans Breitmann did, almost,
And Schnitzerlein gave up the ghost?
'T was all because they could n't boast
My Bicycle.

And saying mine, I do not mean
There are not many others seen
Who ride like me on my machine,
My Bicycle.

I'm not stuck up, tho' seated high;
To ride, at once, and run and fly —
My pride is so to travel by
My Bicycle.

Who will may head with learning stow,
I work the light, ped-antic toe —
'T is *cyclopedic* lore to know
                    My Bicycle.

And when the saddled arc I span,
What care I for the fall of man?
Let him remount! I always can
                    My Bicycle.

All the mutations I discern
Of men and States not me concern,
While I avoid to overturn
                    My Bicycle.

See Russia rotten Turkey eat —
And John Bull in a stewing heat;
We have a better kind of meet,
                    My Bicycle.

Then hurry spokes and spokesman too,
We only have an hour or so,
And almost twenty miles to go,
                    My Bicycle.

TRANSLATIONS VERY MUCH TRANSLATED FROM LONGFELLOW.

THE CELESTIAL CYCLER.

FROM DANTE.

SCENE, *Coast near Boston.*

AND now, behold! as at the approach of morning [*]
Through the gross vapors, Sol grows fiery round,
Down in the east upon the ocean floor,

Appeared to me, — I may alway behold it! —
A wheel along the sea, so swiftly coming,
Its motion by no flight of wing is equalled.

And when therefrom I had withdrawn a little
Mine eyes, that I might question Mr. W–st–n,
Again I saw it brighter grown and larger.

---

[*] I saw from the beach, when the morning was shining,
A *wheel* o'er the waters move gloriously on. — MOORE.

Then on each side of it appeared to me
I knew not what of *legs*, and underneath,
Little, so little! there came forth another.

My mentor yet had uttered not a word,
While the first brightness into wheels unfolded;
But, when he clearly recognized the chariot,

He cried aloud: "Learn, quick, to bow the knee
And hold the handles! Now, get up thy spunk!
Henceforward shalt thou see such bicyclers!

"See, how he scorns all common arguments,
So that no horse he wants, nor other speed
Than his own wheels, between all distant points.

"See, how he holds them, pointed straight to Boston!
Fanning the air with the bicyclic pinions,
That do not moult themselves like mortal hair."

Then, as still nearer and more near us came
The Bird of Britain, more glorious he appeared
On that — the eye could not endure his presence;

But down he cast him, and he came to ground
By a small footstep, gliding swift and light,
So that the cycles wobbled not thereby.

Upon the strand stood Bisakel the Angel!
Beatitude seemed written in his face!
And more than wine-red spirits shone within.

"*In exitu* the Yankees out of Walking!"
Thus sang we three together in one voice,
Like whatso in that Psalm of old is written.

Then made he sign of wheely rood upon us;
Whereat we took the horse-car for the town,
And he sped onward swiftly as he came.

SONG OF THE SILENT WHEEL.

Upon the Silent Wheel!
Ha! who shall lift us thither?
Life in its middle term begins to wither,
And shaky shanks are thinner to the feel.

SONG OF THE SILENT WHEEL.

Who leads us with a gentle zeal
Thither — and whither?
Upon the silent Wheel?

Upon the silent wheel,
Out over boundless regions
Of equitation! Send the mounting legions
Of youthful souls, the future's pledge of weal.
Who miles on axles firm can reel,
Shall be Health's carrier pigeons,
Upon the silent wheel!

On WHEEL and wheel,
To all the book-besotted,
The eldest heralds of the gait allotted
Beckon, and with reverted looks appeal,
To lead us with a gentle zeal
Into the seat of the great imported,
Upon the silent wheel!

THE CYCLE ON THE ROAD.

" HAST thou seen that lordly cycle,
　That Cycle on the Road?
Boldly and glad above it
　The lads float *à la mode.*

" And fain it would flop downward
　To the pebbled road below;
And fain it would sweep onward
　With the fleeting rims aglow."

" Well have I seen that cycle,
　That Cycle on the Road,
And the lads above it treading,
　And the dust rise as they trode."

" The wheels and the boys of Boston,
　Had they a merry time?
Didst thou hear, from those lofty saddles,
　The sharp of their whistles' chime?"

" The wheels and the boys of Boston,
　They came back quietly;

Tho' I heard on the gale no sound of wail,
　　The tears came to mine eye."

"Sped they not back in rapture,
　　Talking of their royal ride?
Resplendent as the morning sun,
　　Beaming with ruddy pride?"

"Well, I saw the young bicyclers,
　　With dust from crown to sandals;
They were moving slow, in weeds of woe —
　　Had been flung over their handles!"

THE EARTH HATH ITS GEMS.

The earth hath its gems,
　　The heaven hath its stars;
But my heart, my heart,
　　My heart hath its wheel.

Great are the earth and the heaven;
　　Yet greater is my heart,
And fairer than gems and stars
　　Flashes and beams my wheel.

Thou little youth, and man, then,
  Come unto my great heart;
My heart, and the earth, and the heaven,
  Are fleeting away with wheels.

THE WHEEL.

"WHITHER, on whirling wheel?
Whither, with so much haste,
As if a thief thou wert?"

"I have the Wheel of life;
Soiled with my city's dust,
From the struggle and the strife
Of the narrow street I fly
To the Road's felicity,
To clear from me the frown
Of the moody toil of town."

(*End of Translations.*)

PEGASUS IN (ABOUT 40) POUND.

Dies rotæ, dies illa.

ONCE into a quiet city,
   Without taste and without feed,
In the golden prime of Autumn,
   Came the Briton's iron steed.

Thereupon, to that age common,
   From the school-boys was abuse;
But the wise men, in their wisdom,
   Put him straightway into use.

Then two morning city papers
   Both allowed his praises well —
Dealers down the street proclaiming
   There were bicycles to sell.

And the curious city people,
   Rich and poor, and old and young,
Came in haste to see this wondrous
   Wheely steed, with wire strung.

PEGASUS IN (ABOUT 40) POUND.

Patiently and still, expectant,
    Waited he of flighty limb,
For disporting far his pinions
    In the triumph meant for him.

Then with circuits wide extended,
    Breaking up their toil and care,
Lo, the strange steed late imported,
    Was familiar everywhere.

And they found within th' Eleventh Ward,
    Where the cycling club had meets,
Pure and bright example flowing
    From the wheeling in the streets.

From that hour, the horse unfailing
    Gladdens the whole region round,
Strengthening all who sit his saddle,
    While he bears them without sound.

THE LADDER OF ST. HYGEIA.

MR. SONGFELLOW, ASSISTED TO NEW ALTITUDES.

WELL, Saint Hygeia, have they said
   That, of devices we can frame,
Your bicycle is best to tread
   For following up a healthy aim.

All common folk to elevate,
   Who wish to quicken and amend —
Its flight of steps, that rolling gait,
   Are rounds by which they may ascend.

The low-back ones, the base design,
   That make had many virtues less;
Its revels here in 'Sixty-nine
   Were all occasions of excess.

The longing for big noble things,
   The time for triumph, now ensu'th,
With hardening of the hand that brings
   Persistence in the ways of youth.

Small draughts of ale — small beers, we need,
   That have their roots in; cause no reel,
And never wobble nor impede
   The action of the sober wheel.

Treadles must now be trampled down
   Beneath our feet, that we may gain
In the bright roads of every town
   The right of evident domain!

Having no wings, we cannot soar;
   But we have feet and hands to climb
By due degrees, by more and more,
   The saddled summits of our time.

The mighty bicycles of John
   Bull wedge-like cleave the suburb airs;
When nearer seen, to gad upon,
   They are like antic flights of stairs

O'er distant green hills that uprear
   Their rounded backs toward the skies,
Crossing by roadways that appear
   As we to higher levels rise.

The seats bicyclers reached and kept,
  Were not secured by sudden flight;
But they, while their companions crept,
  Were toiling — tumbling left and right.

Walking is what was long a bore
  With persons bent on exercise;
We now discern, unseen before,
  The steps to higher destinies.

Nor deem the boneshaker of the past
  Is wholly wasted, wholly vain,
As rising on the Arch at last,
  To cycling nobler we attain.

THE STILLY WHEEL.

BY MR. LONGFELLOE.

Auspice Hygeiâ, et sine labe perfectus.

NOWHERE such a previous steed,
Not in fancy — even, indeed,
'Zekiel saw no wheels with brake
Linked together in their make.

THE STILLY WHEEL.

Man on little leather shelf —
Ever balancing itself,
Goes the wheel so still and fast
That it hardly seems to haste.

Never charioteer of old,
On his oaken axle rolled,
Such a course erect pursued
Through the gazing multitude.

Never school-boy in his zest
For all spinning things the best,
Top, or hoop, or sling, came out
Wandering whirling thus about.

As the mirror of its ride,
People thickly on each side
Hang converted, and between
Floating fly the lads serene.

Hawk or eagle on the wing
Seems the only travelling
Like to one who laughs and flies
On those wheels' contrasted size.

THE STILLY WHEEL.

Silent wheel! that Indian mood
Fame has not misunderstood;
For thou glidest not alone,
Ill content to be unknown.

And thy transits softly teach
Wisdom more than human speech,
Speeding without toil or noise
In unshaken equipoise.

Though it turneth no busy mill,
Yet, so stirring and so still,
Gives some moving words to say
To the traveller on his way:

"Traveller, hurrying from the heat
Of the city, play thy feet!
Ride a wheel, nor longer waste
Life with inconsiderate taste.

"Go not with the crowd that crawls
Where the rattling horse-car hauls,
Sit the quiet nag of steel,
Link together wheel and weal."

BICYCLICALISTHENICS.

BY LONGFELLOW ET AL.

O GRACEFUL one that fleetest on, thy pace
Is an aerial promenade, and thy form
Goes poised as if it floated on the air,
With the soft ambulating gait of one
Who timeth all his motions to a measure!
And has Prometheus, say, has he again
Been stealing fire from Helios' chariot-wheels
To light bicycles with, and make them spin?
Who thinks of bicycling hath already taken
One step upon the way to eminence :
Such altitudes delight me — *I will* launch
On the sustaining wire, nor fear to fall
Like Icarus, nor serve myself like him
Who drove awry Hyperion's fiery steeds.
   O fortunate, O happy day,
   When a new cycle bears its load
   Among the myriad wheels of earth ;
   Like a young moon just spun to birth,

It rolls on its harmonious way
Into the boundless realms of road!

NOTE. — In my first versions of some of the pieces in this volume the effort of the joke was, obviously, to make each poet sing the bicycle as nearly as might be in his own very words, which was curiously possible, especially in those from Longfellow. That aim became afterward but a secondary one, and much is now altered accordingly. The cutting line of the young man at one of the hotels lately, in —

> "Quotation marks are here as thickly strewn
> As ought to be in some poems having none,"

does not apply to the Bi-lyrical muse; though such disfigurement might pass in much simplistic and mere walking poetry, or the sort he was reading on that occasion.

It is quite surprising how easily and largely the verse of our most artistic poet yielded itself to my designs.

'Longfellowing rolls the boom of the white-nickeled wheel.'

YANKEE-LAND.

Novus ordo cyclorum.

THE destined wheel is on thy shore,
    Yankeeland!
Its perch is at thy ample door,
    Yankeeland!
Ascend the gay exotic goer
That flashed the streets of Boston o'er,
And beat the boneshaker of yore,
    Yankeeland, my Yankeeland!

Hark to the wondering son's appeal,
    Yankeeland!
"My mother dear, I want a wheel,"
    Yankeeland!
For life and health, for "go" and weal,
Thy beardless cavalry reveal,
And speed their beauteous limbs with steel!
    Yankeeland, my Yankeeland!

They must not tumble in the dust,
    Yankeeland!
Their beaming steel should never rust,
    Yankeeland!
That slender firmness you may trust
Like slender blades in warlike thrust
Held by those numbered with the just,
    Yankeeland, my Yankeeland!

Come, for the wheel is bright and strong,
    Yankeeland!
Come, for thy carriance does thee wrong,
    Yankeeland!
Come for thy young bard in the throng,

Who stalks with levity along,
And gives a new key to much song,
  Yankeeland, my Yankeeland!

LAY OF THE PEDESTRIAN.

*Stet quicunque volet, potens
Rotæ culmine lubrico.* — SENECA.

TURN, Cycler, turn thy wheel and lower the proud;
Turn thy still wheel past steeds and coaches loud;
 Thy wheel and thee we rather like than hate.

Turn, Cycler, turn thy wheel long miles from town;
With that high wheel we go not up — or down;
 Our speed is little, but our prudence great.

Smile we to see you up in many lands;
Down, and we smile, sure of our feet and hands;
 That wheel we ride not, nor. deride, but wait.

Turn, turn thy wheel above the walking crowd;
Thy wheel and thou are greater than the proud;
 Thy wheel and thee we rather like than hate.

THE BICYCLE.

A. T. +D.

Sure never yet was any heel
  Could flit so lightly by.
Keep off, or else my bicycle
  Will hit you coming nigh.

How lightly whirls the bicycle!
  How fiery-like you fly!
Go, get you one; this ticklish wheel
  Be taught before you try.

Thou darest — give me now to reel
  The rapid miles, or die.
There, take it, take my bicycle
  And break your neck thereby.

———•———

Up! and the dusty race
  That sat in horse-cars long —
Be swift their feet as antelopes,
  And as steam-engine strong.

HASTE NOT, PAUSE NOT.

NEWLY TRANSLATED FROM OLD GOEASY (OFTEN SPELT GOETHE).

WITHOUT pause, without haste!
Print the motto in thy breast;
Bear it with you as a spell
When you ride the bicycle.
Cobblestones may bring you down —
Bear right onward out of town.

Haste not! Let no reckless deed
Mar for aye the slender steed.
Balance well, and keep the right,
Onward then with all delight.
Haste not! Years may ne'er atone
For one "nasty cropper" done.

Pause not! Teams are sweeping by;
Tumble there not, lest you die.
Nothing mighty and sublime
Thus to fall before your time.
Glorious 't is to live to ride,
While these forms of ours abide.

Haste not, pause not! Calmly sit;
Meekly bear a front of grit.
Heed not boys that cry thee "Whoa,
Emma"— let them see thee go.
Duly wag thy pivot guide,
Take the right, whate'er betide.
Haste not, pause not! Trials past,
Health shall crown thy work at last.

THE STEED OF FIRE.

FROM POE'S "ELDORADO"— FABLED GOLDEN MADE
TRUE STEEL.

SOBERLY dight,
A modern knight
Upon a hack of hire
Had journeyed long
Singing a song
In search of a steed of fire.

But he grew old,
This knight, tho' bold,

With o'er his heart a dire
    Dump as he found
    Nothing around
That looked like a steed of fire.

    And as his strength
    Waned, he at length
Met a bicycling flyer:
    "Flyer," said he,
    "What! can it be —
Can this be the steed of fire?"

    "Upon this mount
    We surely count,
'T is all you can desire;
    Ride, boldly ride,"
    Cycler replied,
"If you seek for a steed of fire!"

    He dried his tears, —
    And shed his years,
All on the windy wire;
    And sweeps along
    Singing much song
In praise of the steed of fire.

BISAKEL.

"ISRAFEL," BY POE, RECAST FOR A NEW ROLL.

The angel Bisakel, whose wings are wheels, has the fleetest pace of all God's creatures. — Koran.

In heaven a spirit doth dwell
   Whose great wing is a wheel.
None fly so wildly well
As the angel Bisakel,
And the giddy stars, so legends say,
Slowing their course, attend the play
   Of his wondrous heel.

Maturing her age,
   In her highest noon,
   The enamelled moon
Reddens with rage,
   And to witness, with misgivin',
(With the nautic Pleiads even,
   More than seven,)
   Pauses in heaven.

And they say (the starry choir
   And the other gossiping things)

That Bisakeli's fire
Is owing to that tire
   O'er which he sits and slings
The trembling living wire
   Of those unusual wings.

But surely that angel trod
   Treadles amazing footy;
And, for a grown-up god,
   There the Houris' eyeballs are
His axle bearings — beauty
   Transports faster than a star!

The ecstasies he took
   With such rolling orbs to deal —
His leg and style, his pure caoutchouc,
   With the fervor of his wheel —
   Well may the stars go reel!

We say thou art not wrong,
   Bisakeli, who despisest
Feathers and psalming song;
Bloom thou the laurels among,
   Best angel and, the wisest, —
Merrily live, and long!

— Ah, heaven is his'n, indeed;
This world is sweets *and* sours;
Our powers are puny powers,
And the slowest of his perfect speed
Is the swiftest of ours.

If I could dwell
Where Bisakel
Hath dwelt, and he where I,
He might not spin so wildly well
Our mortal wheelery,
While a better song than now might swell
From my lyre within the sky —
But — how is this "for *high*"?

GRAND CHORUS.

J. D. + D.

AT last great Bisakeli came,
Inventor of the rotal frame;
The fleet enthusiast, from his starry store,
Enlarged the former rattling rounds,
And added height to hushéd sounds,

With Britain's mother-wit, and arts unknown before.
>His new machine deserves the prize,
>To that award the crown;
>It raises mortals toward the skies,
>And draws an angel down.

OWED TO THE BICYCLE.

(AND PAID IN ALTERED NOTES FROM TOM MOORE.)

>It came o'er the sea,
>My Cycle to me,
Came thro' sunshine, storm, and snows;
>Rubber and steel,
>This, the true wheel,
Turns the same where'er it goes.
Tho' fate may frown, so I ride and fall not,
'T is life on the wing, a life that can pall not.
>Thou cam'st o'er the sea,
>Bicycle, to me,
Came whence chilly our east wind blows;
>Seas may congeal,
>But the true wheel
Turns the same where'er it goes.

Was not the sea
Made to bring thee?
Land for roads and rides alone?
Once walking slaves,
Cycle us saves, —
Wheel and liberty's all our own.
No fare to pay, no limits to bound us,
The town behind, and the country around us —
Thou cam'st o'er the sea,
Bicycle, to me,
Came thro' sunshine, storm, and snows;
Seas may congeal,
But thy true wheel
Turns the same, where'er it goes!

THOSE BICYCLES.

IN MIDSUMMER.

THOSE bicycles, those bicycles!
How merry a tale their image tells,
Of youth and health, and that fleet time
When last I heard their whistle's chime.

Those boyous hours are passed away;
And many a heart that then was gay,
Out of or in town darkly dwells,
And rides not now those bicycles.

Again 't will be — they are not gone;
That gleeful wheel will still roll on,
While I help bards to *wire* their shells
And sing your praise, fleet bicycles.

ANACREON: ODE XXXIX.

MO(O)RE TRANSLATED THAN EVER.

How I love the restive boy,
Tripping on the wheel of joy!
How I love the mellow sage,
Rolling up the hill of age!

And whene'er the man of years
On the wheel of boy appears,
Snows may o'er his head be hung,
But his heart and heels are young.

ROTAL POESY.

BY T. W. O.

Who comes so rollicking,
  Riding along,
While the blue poetess
  Frets at his song?
Song, she says, vying
With the high crying
Wild geese in flying
  Samely prolong.

Not so the ragged boy
  By the wayside,
Watching that bicycle
  Down the road glide,
Wire bird winging,
Thro' the dust bringing
That rhymer singing
  To the hushed ride.

"Stay," said the little boy,
  "Bicycle, stay;
Linger, sweet ballader,
  Linger, I say."

Swiftly proceeding
Past both, unheeding,
Song and wheel speeding
Glided away.

So to all youthful eyes
    Bicycles shone ;
Every bard able was
    Forced to get on,
Editors declining
Some things combining
Two in one shining.
    Who's the next one?

FROM THE GREEK.

BY T. M. + D.

If you ride upon horses or asses,
    You'll never write anything nice ;
The wheel's the true steed of Parnassus,
    Which carries a bard to the skies.

THE DANDY BICYCLER.

Cyclus Scintillans.

RICH and fair were the wheels he sat,
And he had on his head a strange club hat;
But his gay leggings were far beyond
His sparkling spokes or level wand.

"Laddy! dost thou not fear to stray
Alone, bicycling through this by-way?
Are Erin's sons so peaceable grown
As not to be tempted to throwing the stone?"

"Old man, I feel not the least alarm,
No son of Erin will offer me harm;
For though they love mischief and rows galore,
Old man, they love manly exertion more."

On he went there, more than a mile,
In safety, and bright as their own green isle;
And wholly correct is he who relied
Upon Cycle's glamour — and Erin beside.

LITTLE MISS LOQUITUR.

BY T. W. O.

WHENAS on wheels my Johnny goes,
Then, then methinks, how fleetly shows
That lively action of his hose.

And when I cast mine eyes and see
What brave vibration wires be,
Oh, how that glittering taketh me!

"MUSIC" ON THE WIRE.

WM. STRODE, ABOUT 1630, — NOW RIDES.

WHEN seniors tread the cranky wheel,
   From creeping passing to that art,
And when at every turn we feel
   Our pulses stir and bear a part;
     When wires can make
     The heartstrings wake;
     Philosophy
     Cannot deny
   The wheel is made of jollity.

When with excursive boys we train,
　　Where'er the wheel affecteth most;
And sometimes singing, will maintain
　　Bicyclers mid the heavenly host, —
　　　　In lays we think
　　　　Make poets blink;
　　　　Philosophy
　　　　Cannot deny
　　The wheel consists of jollity.

Thus did the flighty bicycle
　　My senses rock with motion sweet;
Like wool * on snow its paces fell,
　　Soft like a spirit's, and as fleet.
　　　　Grief who needs feel
　　　　That hath a wheel?
　　　　Up let him hie,
　　　　And clambering fly,
　　And change his dole for jollity.

———♦———

UNLESS hereby above himself he can
Erect himself, how poor a thing is man!

---

* *Laneos pedes.*

ROTA ANGLICA.

BY MR. JINGLEBOSOM.

O WHEEL of wire, misjudged by walking man, —
   The power of John Bull's pace,
What rides are here since thou and Jonathan
   First greeted face to face!
He doomed to creep, thou on him didst impress
The pattern of a ruddy wheeliness.

'Yes, it was well; for so, mid cares that rule
   Us men to business tied,
The charm uplifts us from the chair and stool
   To seats before untried.
We wheel our course like pigeons or like hawks;
Who rides with us he flies, he is but dust who walks.

THE WHEEL-SHOP.

YOUNG Sixty went there, and soon met with a Friend;
Folks say in his tights he's now going on end!
Then why should not I the same method pursue,
And quicken my paces as other boys do?

                              Forty.

CARMEN BICYCLICUM.

BY T. W. O.

BICYCLING bloods go forth to war
   Hygeia's crown to gain;
Her rosy banner streams afar, —
   Who follows in their train?

Who best can sit his pig-skin perch,
   Triumphant over bane,
Who patient bears his jolt or lurch,
   He follows in their train.

That lawyer first, whose eagle eye
   Could look beyond the law,
Rode forty miles upon the fly,
   Wrote what he did and saw;

And one who raids it into Song,
   'Midst some immortal strain,
Rewriting poets where they 're wrong;
   Who follows in their train?

A glorious band, the chosen club,
  On whom the spirit came,
Twelve valiant saints, their hope the Hub
  Would mock not at the same;

They met the Briton's burnished steel,
  The Lion's narrow wain;
They bowed their necks to mount the wheel, —
  Who follows in their train?

This mobile band of men and boys,
  With many converts made,
Around the State unthrown rejoice,
  In garments light arrayed.

They climbed the steep ascent to saddle
  Thro' trifling toil and pain;
May all yet have the grace to paddle
  And follow in their train!

———•———

BENEATH the roll of men on-tirely great
The Wheel is mightier than the Horse.

FLEET WHEEL.

"SWEET HOME" MADE MORE MOVING.

WITH coaches and palace-cars though we may deal,
Be it even to tumble, there's no seat like wheel!
A charm from the skies ever follows us there,
Which, riding enclosed, is not met anywhere.
   Wheel, wheel, fleet wheel!
   There's no seat like wheel!

Apart from the wheel, metals dazzle in vain!
O give me my high, burnished 'cycle again!
The boys mounting gayly that came at the call;
O give me fleet pace of leg, dearer than all!
   Wheel, wheel, fleet wheel!
   There's no seat like wheel!

WHAT TO DO.

IF sad that Fortune's wheel can't use thee well,
And seeking for some surer "dear Gazelle,"
Cheer up, step up, and try the bicycle.

HIS FIRST RIDE.

*By Sir Frightful Plagiary
Taken from Miss Alice Carey.*

EARTH with its slow and tiresome ills
   Recedes some feet away;
Lift up y'r heads, ye neighboring hills,
   I'm coming out your way!

My soul is full of pilfered song,
   *Highway*man's is my right;
Bicycles that I feared too long,
   Are things of life — and light.

My pulses fast and fearless beat,
   My limbs seek wider bounds,
I feel grow firm beneath my feet
   The rubber pedal rounds.

A Fifty-inch the courage gives
   High as the brave to go;
Same force in my two-wheeler lives,
   Our circulations show.

This is the safe and narrow way —
    The wires sing in the wind —
To men on horse of flesh I say,
    I 've no such carnal mind.

In palace-cars I would not be,
    Where rides the railroad king;
O steam, where is thy victory?
    O bird, where is thy wing?

N. B. — He came a nasty cropper and back by rail!

"MORTALITY" ENLIVENED.

*Made from William Knox's song,
Twice as true, and half as long.*

WHY should not the spirit of mortal be proud?
Like a fast fleeting meteor, a fast flying cloud,
The sweep of the foam on the crest of a wave,
He passes from town on his bicycle brave!

The lad on whose cheek, on whose brow, in whose eye,
Shine beauty and pleasure — he triumphs to fly;

And the memory of those boneshakers once praised
Is away from the minds of the lively erased.

So the two-wheeler goes, like the flourishing weed,
That withers away to let flowers succeed;
So the two-wheeler comes — even those we behold,
To reseat every tail on the bicycle bold.

We are not the same sort that our fathers have been,
Nor see the same sights that our fathers have seen;
We drink the same stream, and we feel the same sun,
But run *not* the same *course* that our fathers have run.

The thoughts we are thinking, could our fathers think?
From "Spirits" we're not shrinking from, how they did shrink!
To the wheel we are clinging to, they too would cling,
For it speeds on the road like a bird on the wing.

They died — without Ride! had they things we have now,
Who race on the turf that lies over their brow,
They'd made in their dwellings a transient abode,
To have bicycle-meets on their pilgrimage road.

'Tis the wink of an eye, 't is the wag of a tail,
To the blossom of health from the drudgery pale, —
From the gilded saloon of the beer and the crowd —
Why should not the mortal of spirit be proud?

SONG TO BISAKEL.

(*Deus ex Machinâ.* The Prince of Pace.)

To Bisakel we sing to-day,
Whose steely beams with fancy play,
And make his wheels so brightly shine
Aurora's face is less divine.
Sing him, and to the sliding throne
Of sparkles which he goes upon.
    Io Pæans let us sing,
    No physic! Bisakel is king.

Sound all his praises with right fire,
Captive bards support the lyre;
With laurelled helmet for his head,
Disciples dance about his tread;

When on his rushing wire he plays,
Scatter roses round, and bays.
   Io Pæans let us sing
   To the bright pedalian king.

WHERE'S MY JOHN?

BY T. W. O.

"Ho, Cycler from the road!
Where's my boy — my boy?"
"What's the boy's name, good wife,
And what is the make he strode?"

"My boy John —
He that went to ride —
What! I'm not on the 'make,' Cycler;
My boy, my boy's my pride.

"You come back to town,
And not seen my John?
I might as well have asked some hodman
Down there in the town.
There's not your likes in all the county,
But he knows my John.

WHERE'S MY JOHN?

"Where's my boy — my boy?
Speak louder, and let me know,
Or I swear you are no cycler,
Tight breeches or no,
Gay leggings or no, Cycler,
Whistle and such or no!
Sure his'n is called a Jolly Briton."

"He rode too fast, too fast."
"And why should I be fast, Cycler?
That have my own boy John!
If I was stout as I am proud
I'd bang you over the crown!
Where's my boy, my John, Cycler?"
"That big wheel went down."

"Where's my boy — my boy?
What care I for the wheel, Cycler?
I was never a-top it.
Be it running or on the ground,
Whether or no, though, I'll be bound,
My Johnny wouldn't swap it.
I say, where's my John?"
"Every man on wheels goes down,
When a man can't stop it."

"Where's my boy — my boy?
What care I for the *men*, Cycler?
That am John's mother!
Where's my boy — my boy?
Tell me of him, and no whopper."
"*He came a* NASTY CROPPER!"

NOTE. — The original of the above seemed well worth capturing, in spite of the severe verdict (in another connection) of a brother rhymer in a New York paper: —

"The fellah th-that steals from Sydney Dobell
Is a wegular lunatic."

A charge of cruelly kidnapping an only child might hold. Methinks I hear a wailing voice, —

Ho, rider of the B!
Where's my poem — my poem?

———◆———

CAREFUL SENIOR'S SONG.

Dum vivimus volvamus.

ENGLAND — how wide her glory shines,
  How high her seats arise!
Known thro' the earth by thousand signs,
  By two signs in the skies.

CAREFUL SENIOR'S SONG.

Bicyclus thence, that art the best,
   The true and living wheel,
Upborne upon that buoyant crest,
   No feebleness I feel.

Quickened thereon, and made alive,
   I equitate afoot;
My life I from thy top derive,
   My vigor from the shoot.

Grafted on thee I reach the sky —
   At least, I think I will,
For seated more than four feet high,
   My soul mounts higher still.

Careful throughout Ward Elev'n I drove,
   From all destruction free;
My hands were well engaged above,
   My legs were still with thee.

Too long, alas, my devious feet
   The sidewalk ways have trode;
Henceforth I'll travel in the street,
   O wheel, or on the road.

CAREFUL SENIOR'S SONG.

My walking beams were feeble sticks,
    Slower and shorter* then;
I was, before, but five feet six,
    And now I'm five feet ten!

Yet many tread a higher crank,
    All modest is my zeal,
I make the limits of my shank
    The bounds unto my wheel.

I clip high-climbing thoughts at sight
    Of rounds of swelling pride;
Their fate is worse that from the height
    Of sixty inches slide.

When cobblestones and crossings show
    Like breakers unto me,
I do whatever I can do,
    And leave the rest to thee.

If casual falls retard our pace,
    Together we arise;
Quickly I reassume my place,
    And ride for exercise.

---

* Four years ago "Mr. Punch" queried as to the growing diameter of the wheel and its effects on length of limb in the future.

THE PILGRIM.

BY SIR WALTER ROLLY.

GIVE me my bicycle of quiet,
My horse of health to walk upon;
Enough of not pultaceous diet, —
My tin of lubrication;
My hose and breeches (leg's true gauge);
And thus I'll take my pilgrimage.
Then every happy day I beg
   More paceful pilgrims I may see,
That have cast off their nags of leg,
   And ride a-wheelback, just like me.

THE LIGHT OF THE STUD.

BICYCLE's the sun of our stable,
   His beams the spokes so fine;
We planets that so are able
   With him to roll and shine.
Let circling mirth abound;
   We'll all grow bright
   With *borrowed* light,
And shine as he goes round.

THE WHEELLESS.

CLOSELY AFTER HOLMES.

WE count the working heads that rest
   Where the fleet whirling riders beckon,
But, on our silent carrier's crest,
   The slow-goers who will stop to reckon?
A few can twirl the magic wire,
   And noiseless wheel is proud to win them;
Alas, for those who walk and tire,
   And bide with all their riding in them!.

Nay, care not for the live alone,
   Much song has told their art's glad story;
Wail for the wheelless, who have none —
   No lyric chants pedestrian glory!
And while Arcadian breezes sweep
   O'er Bicycle's mirific flyer,
Call where the clattering horse-cars creep,
   To bring your brothers *one yard higher:*

"O men that walk, and take car line —
   Have tightening boot or tortoise horses,

And Gout going home to cordial wine,
  Slow-dropped from crowding's crushing process;
Attend the song and echoing chord, —
  With over-ridden poets dealing,
For you the parodies are poured,
  As mad as mirth, as *two* as wheeling!"

A HYMNLET.

Beati possidentes.

HAPPY are we whose joys abound
  High on the whirling rim,
Who Bicycle indeed have found,
  And give the praise to him.

I leave the earth, I rise and go,
  To be upheld and blest;
His'n are both my soles below,
  And that within my breast.

Long may we tread the rapid wheel
  With undiverted feet;
And strength subdue, and flaming zeal,
  The steepest grades we meet.

SOLILOQUY OF A WARY WOBBLER.

ADDISON WITH ADDITIONS.

— Whence this pleasing hope, this fond desire,
This longing after rides on bicycles?
And whence this secret dread and inward horror
Of falling in the mud? Why shrinks the soul
Back on herself, and starts at nasty croppers?
'T is the Divinity that stirs within us,
'T is Bisakel himself points what we 're after,
And intimates bicycling unto man, —
Bicycling, that so pleasing, dreadful thought!

THE PHANTOM OF DELIGHT.

A WORDSWORTHY VARIATION BY A RYDAL BARD.

It was a phantom of delight
When first it gleamed upon my sight;
A lively apparition sent,
To captivate a continent.

THE PHANTOM OF DELIGHT.

Its spokes as rays of starlight fair;
Like starlight, too, they twinkled where
Bestriders hereabout were borne,
From May-time until Christmas morn;
A stately shape, a racer gay,
To mount, to start, and win the day.

I saw it upon nearer view,
A horse, and yet a carriage, too!
With foot-hold motions light and free,
And steps to aid agility.
Accounts are had — in which we meet
Fleet records, promises as fleet;
A creature not too bright to scoot
For human nature's daily foot;
For transient trips, or ample miles,
Onward Rotator tears, and smiles.

And now I feel with hand serene
The very pulse of the machine;*
A being, breathing though no breath,
A traveller e'en for life and death,

---

* William's own line, of dubious fitness till now.

With rider firm, of temperate will,
Of balance, eyesight, strength, and skill;
A perfect carriage, nobly planned
To run with comfort, at command;
And yet a courser still and bright,
Of forty pounds of pure delight.

IN RUNNING'EM & CO.'S SALESROOM.

BY TWO RYDAL BARDS.

"Tax not the rotal Gait with vain expense,
With ill-matched wheels the Artisan who planned
(At first contriving for a jaunty band
Of tight-breeched Britons only) these immense,
And little, whirls of still circumference!
Give all thou canst, my best expect no lower,
The price is regulated less or more."
So spake who sold for merely dollars and cents
These lofty spinners, that launching seat aloof,
Self-poised to shoot over the hills and dells
Where light and shade refresh, where Rustic dwells.
Fingering and pondering them as both would fly,
Our thoughts flew with a fleetness giving proof
That we were born for high legerity.

HYGEIA'S WHEEL.

Lux ecce surgit ferrea.

SWIFT heralds bright
With feet of might
Upon bicycles stand,
   Sent to proclaim
   In John's high name
Glad ridings to the land.
   Long miles they rove,
   They walk above,
And "Come up hither!" cry,
   "The soles that climb
   Wheel's height sublime
Catch Health upon the fly."

   The little child,
   Who brightly smiled
When red three-wheeler bore,
   Will leave that kind, —
   His growing mind
Rides upon something more.
   With accents sweet
   His lips repeat

The chorus of the high :
"True soles that be
From walk made free
Catch Health upon the fly."

Joy crowns our powers
Some summer hours,
And spring and autumn days;
'Mid winter snows
We in repose
Sing thoughts of rolly pace.
Thus pales or burns
Wheel's star by turns,
As rolling seasons fly;
Both Winter's blight
And Summer's light
See bloom upon the Bi.

From health amiss
To height of this
When willing mortals strive,
Wheel is their gain,
And pace amain
Shall keep their blood alive.

But higher still,
O'er trouble's hill,
Their force shall onward hie ;
Till souls shall save
Beyond the grave
Their Health above the sky.

A MERRY CAR.

BY SMITH ET AL.

BICYCLE, 't is of thee,
Fleet car of levity,
   Of thee I sing :
Wheel I and brothers ride,
And on the still rim's pride,
Up every high hill-side
   Drive the great ring.

Two-wheeler — or if three,
Car of hilarity,
   The same I love ;

A MERRY CAR.

I hate the rocky ills
That give me ugly spills,
Yet my heart rather thrills —
  See as above.

Make carols on the breeze,
And wring from all the P's
  Fleet wheeldom's song:
Let walking ones awake,
Let older gents partake,
And, ready on the brake,
  Fly down along!

Our Bisakel, to thee,
Angel of wheelery,
  To thee we sing:
Long make our band be bright
With wheeldom's rolly light;
Propel us by thy might,
  Great pedal king.

ELDERS, COME UP.

J. D. + D.

CREEP ye no more, grave walkers,
   Why need you move so slow?
Look now, the young wheel-stalkers —
   And have n't they got the go!
But though sons easily rise,
   Father still keeping
   Sidewalks hies creeping,
Dully, yet dully hies
           Creeping.

Wheel is a care-beguiling,
   A ride that years befits;
Doth not the son go smiling
   When fair on saddle he sits?
Ride you then, ride and rise,
   Doubt not in feeling
   While he flies wheeling;
Softly, now softly flies
           Wheeling.

TO MIDDEL AGER, ESQ.

J. D. + D.

Least of a bird, sublimely when you might
Fly long and steep, to fail before the height!
What if your dull forefathers did not fly,
Could you not let a bad example die?
Wheelmen are risen into an airier way;
Your age does better to ride fast and gay.
Good sense, then, in your worship would appear,
Now to begin, and so go through the year.

WINTRY MUSINGS.

Habitus Bicyclicus.

When breezes are soft, and roads are hard,
   (Bicycle high with the slippery seat)
Thou to my trying dost give reward,
   · And wheel is my wheel for any meet.

WINTRY MUSINGS. 83

For the drinking and eat of the day,
    (Bicycle high with the slippery seat)
Oft am I bothered and scarce can pay,
    But wheel is my wheel for other meet.

When I, lone bachelor once, did sigh,
    (Bicycle high with the slippery seat)
Thou didst me pity, and drew me nigh
    To wheel as my wheel for partner meet.

When I, since married for my sins, did cry,
    (Bicycle high with the slippery seat)
Again didst pity, and made me fly!
    And wheel is my wheel for true helpmeet.

'T is winter time now, the year is young,
    (Bicycle high with the slippery seat)
My ridings fail me, but may be sung,
    For wheel is my wheel for singing meet.

White as the snow is thy nickeled skin,
    (Bicycle high with the slippery seat)
Though I can't drive it thro' thick and thin,
    The wheel is my wheel for surface meet.

My face paleth, my tread is low,
　(Bicycle high with the slippery seat)
I merely sing you, but travel slow
　Till wheel is my wheel for early meet.

ADAPTED ODE.

THE TRYING 'CYCLER TO HIS WHEEL.

Rotal bird of travelling fame,
Let me quit this sort of game:
Climbing, toppling, faltering, vying,
Oh the strain, the hopes of trying!
Peace, fond motor, cease the strife,
And start me languid into life.

Hark! they whistle; 'cyclers say,
Brother, *spin it right away.*—
This is what abducts me quite!
Steels my sinews, rears my height,
Downs my troubles, stirs my pride;
High-metalled steed, is this your ride?

The town recedes — it disappears!
Fields open on my eyes, my ears
With sounds viatic ring.
On end, with wings, I dance, I fly!
O horse, where is thy quick go-by?
Of chafe where is the sting?

"MY LOVE," A SPOOPSY POEM.

BY PROF. HIGHWELL.

Not as some other wheelers are
  Is she that to my sole is dear;
Her glorious fabric came from far,
Beneath the silver morning star,
  To get her art in over here.

Great felloes hath she of her own,
  Which lesser wheels may never know;
John giveth them to her alone,
And fleet they are as any one
  Direction winds may choose to blow.

But of herself she standeth not,
    Though many can not half so fair;
That simplest duty is forgot, —
Yet hath she no dim rusty spot
    That doth not in her nickel share.

She hath no scorn of common folks,
    And though she is of other birth,
Roundly her axle twirls, and spokes,
And patiently she bears the jokes,
    And rides the Yankee paths of earth.

Blessing she is; John made her so,
    And deeds of daily wheeliness
Roll from her noiseless as the snow, —
Nor will she ever chance to know
    That I'm a jackass, more or less.

A HEADER.

Going leg after leg,
    (As the dog went to Dover)
When he came to a stone,
    Down he went over.

ROTA FELIX.

BEAUMOUNT & FLEETCHER.

Come, Wheel, and with thy fleet reprieving,
   Rock me in delight awhile ;
   Let some pleasing roads beguile
   My reflections, so from thence
   They may take an influence
All my sours of care relieving.

Though but a skeleton a-gliding,
   Life it brings for man or boy!
   Walkers suffer long annoy,
   Ill content with any thought
   In their laggard fancy wrought :
Be mine the joys that come of riding!

"GONDOLA" MADE BICYCLE.

BY LORD BOYRUN.

Didst ever see a Bicycle? For fear
   You have not, I'll describe it you exactly :
'T is an uncovered car that's common here,
   Steered at the front, built lightly but compactly,

Rode by one rider, not called bicyclier;
    They glide along the highway looking crackly,
Just as a witch clapt on a broom can go it,
While some can't make out how it is they do it.

And up and down the avenues they go,
    And over the macadam shoot along,
By day and night, all paces, swift or slow,
    And round the suburbs here, an able throng;
They ply no whip nor spur — and know no whoa,
    As not to them do woful things belong,
For all times they maintain a deal of fun,
Like wedding coaches when the mischief's done.

RHYMES OF THE ROAD.

BY LORD BOYRUN.

I.

Horses we hire no further; and the rays
Of bright wheels make sufficient holidays:
Eloping past the green fields, trees and flowers,
We, shining like the crawling brook, go by.

Clear as its current ride the glowing hours
With a calm vigor, which, tho' to the eye
Idlesse it seem, hath its own industry.
If from the billowy we learn to dive,
'T is bicycle should teach us how to fly;
It bears no flutterers, company can give
No fellow aid — alone, man with his wheel must strive.

II.

WHEEL of the many-twinkling spokes! whose charms
Are all extended up from legs to arms;
Bicycle! though too long boneshaker made —
Reproachful term, bestowed but to upbraid —
Now Phœnix and a volant miracle,
Flashing to view, immense but movable;
Henceforth in all the steel of brightness shine,
The least a vaster than in 'Sixty-nine.
Far be from thee and thine the name of rude;
Though yet triumphant, be our ways subdued.
Our legs most move to conquer as they fly,
If wheels and hopes are reasonably high.

SONNETS

BY WHEELIAM SHAKESPOKE.

TO ABEL ELDER.

Insistere rotis.

I. (7)

WHEN from the orient graceful Carrier light
Sported his well-turned limbs, each under eye
Made image of the new-appearing sight,
Serving with gaze his saddled ministry.
An thou hadst climbed the steep-up Bicycle,
Resuming strong youth in thy middle age,
Yet-middling looks to his were semblable,
Amending on his steely pilgrimage;
But when of highmost wheel, with wary care
Like feeble age, thou reelest from the ray,
Thine eyes, 'fore Gad, man! now perverted are
From his high act to seek the nether way:
So, thou thyself low-going in thy noon,
Look for no rise, unless thou get thee one.

II. (16)

THEN wherefore do not you an airy way
Make speed to shun this stealthy tiger, Time,
And 'forty-pound' yourself against decay?
Which means light one of fifty inch to climb!
Now stand you on the top of happy cranks,
And many centric sinews stiffly set,
A stable horse, would bear your lively shanks,
Much better than the panting counterfeit.
So should the hues of life that lift repair;
While toilet's pencil, or my truthful pen,
Neither in phys'nomy nor tract of hair,
Can draw you like yourself made young again:
To ride away yourself keeps yourself still,
And you most live, drawn by your own fleet skill.

THE REASONS WHY.

Alto ex Bicycli vertice.

I. (76)

WHY is my verse so fertile of new ride,
So full of levitation and quick range?

And all the time why do I prance astride
Of goodliest authors and make compounds strange?
Why write I still of one (over the same),
And laud invention in a noted steed,
With very words in almost every name,
Showing their worth where higher to proceed?
Know ye, big bards, I love to link with you, —
One great, one small wheel, on the road have led;
So all my zest is spinning old song new,
Speeding again what is already sped.
Just like the riding rod I daily hold,
So is my pen con-trolling what is trolled.

II. (59)

SAY there be nothing new, but that which is
Was old before, should be their brains reviled
Who, laboring with invention, bore in this
The second burden of a buried child?
O that could record with a rearward look
Of many hundred circuits of the sun
Show the like image in some antique book,
Or prediluvian print in fossil done!
That I might see what in that world made way
For the combinèd meteors of this frame;

What they ascended, if slow or faster they,
Or wheely revolution be the same :
Then might I claim from wits of every time
The self-same right to reconstructed rhyme.

TO BISAKEL.

Cantilenam eandem canens.

I. (78)

OFTEN have I invoked thee for my muse,
And found a rare persistence in the verse,
Where every salient pen serveth my use,
And under thee our poesy disperse.
Thy rays that warmed the dumb on high to sing,
And heavy ambulance aloft to fly,
Have added wires to the poets' string,
And given grace to dual wheelery.
Thou art the guide of that which I compile,
Fair-spoken wheels and words belong to thee ;
Of others' works thou dost amend the style,
Their arts with thy fleet races racy be :
'T is thou art all my art, and dost advance
To vie with William my full countenance.

II. (38)

How can my mind want matter to invent,
While there are books, and thou pour'st into verse
Thine own fleet betterment, too highly bent
For every vulgar paper to rehearse?*
Then give thyself no care — if aught I see
Worthy bestowal, and to gain thy right,
Am not so dumb I cannot sing of thee,
Who hast thyself given us invention light;
Thou, the tenth Muse, in these times more in worth
Than those old nine which my bards invocate.
And he still harping on, let him set forth
Their subject numbers to outlive his date.
If my light-fingering please these carious days,
The stealth be mine, but thine the wealth and praise.

SHAKESPOKE'S EPIGRAM.

Young friend, for cyclus' sake forbear
To bite the dust that 's ever near.
Blest is the man avoids the stones,
And curst is he that breaks his bones.

---

* William's own line; some editors afeard!

THE BICYCLER; A VAGARY.

(Writer been taking something.)

HEARTI- and hardiness unite
   To give Bicycler's name a raise ;
Most fairly seen in the clear light
   That fills 'excursions of two days.'

A knightly character he bears —
   Not that his business office knows ;
Unfading is the coat he wears,
   If first-class tailor makes his clothes.

Cock of the walk for treading high,
   Elation shines upon his face —
His coat, I say, is the real dye —
   His steps are levity and graçe.

Inferior horses he disdains,
   Nor stoops to lower walks on earth ;
John Taurus' goodly work maintains
   The expanses of his airy mirth.

The stoutest gent who struts below,
   When trained to fill a seat above,
John gives him all he can bestow,
   His wheeldom of diurnal move.

Beer shall be lavished at the halt —
   Methinks from earth I see him rise!
Clubbers convulse to see him vault,
   And shout him welcome to the wise!

CAMPBELL, UNDONE AND OUTDONE.

WHEN oftentimes the young aerial beau
Spans on bright arch the glittering wheels below,
Why to yon upland turns the 'cycling eye,
Whose misty outline mingles with the sky?
Why do those tracts of soberer tint appear
More meet than all the landscape shining near?
'T is *distance* sends enchantment to his view,
And lures the mounted with its azure hue.

ALTA CANENS.

TO THE SURVIVING EIGHT OF THE FORTY.

BY T. W. O.

SWEET poets of this move!
   Who sing, without design,
The song of artful love,
   In unison with mine;
These echoing lays contain
   Full many notes of ours
Which you ones cannot gain
   With less than boosted powers.

The wheel of nickeled charms
   ~~These~~ *Such* hearts too seldom love,
Although the treadle warms
   And lightens all above.
How slow their classic things
   To this our modern lot,
High-layrious Mount with springs,—
   And yet they seek them not!

Bi-writing cannot rest
  Till rhymsters so improve,
That, reading and distrest,
  Ye bards will join the move:
'T is happy, with its brakes
  Beneath the chastening hand;
But, doubtless, no great shakes
  If you can't understand.

APOLOGY.

Qui facit per alium facit per se.

THAT which I sing is partly mine,
Dear son of Song, remade of thine;
When thou hast learned to ride, shalt see
The perfect meaning found by me.

That song I made, it was not mine
When fraught with incense superfine,
Till, when thou sang'st it sweetly through,
I with my voice sang — making two.

All which I am, it is not mine:
The moon unto the earth doth shine —
Not of herself, but every ray
Quotes from a bright One far away.

NON ASSUMPSIT.

YOUNG Rollo sat riding a wheel with his foot,
  And he sang, "Will you come on the Flyer?"
Tall middle-aged man had stood hitherto mute,
And now turned away, like an indolent brute,
  And he said, "I'll not come any higher."

    IT is a little wheel
    All of rubber and steel,
With a big one, rather fickle, on afor'ard;
    And when it is good,
    It is very very good,
But when it is bad, it is horrid!

WHEELY THOUGHTS AND EJACULATIONS.

ROTALIS EQUITATUS.

OH who can forget the first rides, after learning,
    When wheeling gave life a new edge with its steel;
And the soul, like those cakes made delicious by
    turning,
    Gave out all its sweets up a-top of the wheel!

Forth going in beauty from nation to nation,
    Most lively and fleet its dominion shall be;
Big poets proclaim it the best equitation,
    And to roll ever on like the waves of the sea.

WESTWARD the horse Bicycle takes its way;
    The four-foot one already passed,
Now swiftly goes the charmer with the day:
    John's noblest offspring is his last.

ARE YOU READY?

ARE you ready for the meeting
  With bicyclers in the air?
Longing for that wheely greeting
  With the handsome many there?
If not ready, if not steady,
  Oh, for that great way prepare!

WHEN I was young, and in my prime,
I used to foot it all the time;
But now I'm old and getting gray,
I ride bicycle every day.

ONE self-propelling hour whole days outshines
Of vapid walkers, or of horse-car lines;
And more true joy bicycler axled feels
Than driver with a trotter to his wheels.

HEREDITARY walkers! know ye not
Who would be free, themselves must mount the
  wheel?

SLICK TRANSIT GLORIA BICYCLI.

Our airy feet with well known flight,
    Swift on the twinklings of the wire,
Run up the hills that heave in sight,
    And leave the walking world to tire.

Cleave to the earth, ye booted ones,
    Contented kick your native dust!
While old bicyclers and their sons
    Light-footed tread the wheel they trust.

'T is the morning of life gives bicyclical lore,
And coming wheels *can* cast their riders before.

In currente rotâ qui sedet, pervolat terram.

Health and joy and youth returning,
    Here have fixed their leather seat;
With Bisakel our hearts are burning,
    He is with us when we meet.

EVEN on this wheel come all who can,
And leave behind them the old man.

A TYPE in nature for bicycling souls, —
Rivers can only run, great Ocean rolls!

WHAT is it makes best bicycles so light?
Because they 're nickeled of a glossy white.

EACH on his narrow seat of porcine hide,
The gay forefathers of the future ride.

Post equitem sedet atra cura
Doth not apply to the 'cycling tourer.

WHILE the wheel holds out to turn,
The *milest* walker may go learn.

POEM OF THE RIDE.

A PARODY-MOSAIC.

BY WALT WHEELMAN.

Poetica surgit tempestas.

1. SEATED, but erect, I take to the open road,
Sturdy, free, the wheel beneath me,
The long brown path before me, leading wherever I choose.

2. Allons! Whoever you are, come travel with me!
Travelling with me, you find what never tires.
Omnes! en masse, Americanos! Libertad! Respondez!
I am he that walks on the rigid and rolling wheel;
I call to the rolling earth and sea, upheld by the wheel,
Wheel of the wiry quietude! Wheel of the small many spokes!
Slim, trim, glossy, peculiar wheel! Mad, gentle, skeleton, rubber, nickel wheel!

POEM OF THE RIDE.

Behold the great rondure, all bright from central to
    extreme — the cohesion of all, how perfect!
The fine centrifugal spokes of light, the quick, tremulous whirl of the wheels — the two wheels, twain but not twin.

3. I chant the chant of rotation or ride, a ride with a
    flying flavor;
We have had crawling and perambulating about
    enough.
I show that wheel is only development.
From this hour, freedom, and a sprightly domination!
From this hour, we ordain ourselves loosed of limits
    and all horse-car lines,
Going where we list — our own motors, rotal and
    resolute.

4. Here is realization, the requisite realization of
    health;
Here is a man rallied, and he fires up what he has in
    him.
Sublimed upon the zenith of a wheel, I ride the triumphal arch of hygienic hilarity.

I tread the pedal orbits with plunging feet;
I dance and equilibrize on the revoluting stilts;
Trampling strong to the hill-tops, and shooting the rapids down.
My foothold is tenoned and mortised in confidence,
And I know the amplitude of space.
Mine is the wheel of the most high, a sixty-incher.
Earth! you seem to look for something at my feet;
Say, old Stop-not! what do you want?
Far-swooping, whirling Earth, with the trailing satellite,
Smile, for your Bicycler comes! We it is who balance ourselves, orbic and stellar.
We must have a turn together — beat the gong of revolution for our rouse and early start.

5. Long had I walked my cities, my country roads and farms, only half-satisfied.
I heard what was said of the universe, its immensities of space and time, its orbits of stars and planets, its chronological, geological and astronomical cycles;
It is middling well as far as it goes, — But is that all?

Belonging to the winders of the circuit of circuits, my words are words of a questioning, and to indicate rotality and motive-power.
I know perfectly well my own Iegotism;
One of that centripetal and centrifugal band, full of the power of the wheely boast, I turn and talk like an engine blowing off steam after a journey.

6. I rise elastic through all, sweep with the true levitation,
The whirling of wheeling elemental and primeval within me;
In a higher walk of life, an unearthly walk.
That I ride and speak is spectacle enough for the great authors and schools — me imperturbe, aplomb, orotund, turbulent, emerging superb.
I harbinge, I promulge, I propound haughty and gigantic enigmas.
I step up to say I am a Chaos, a pied marauder on the rampage!
I sound my sarcastic whoop over the bardic habitudes — rhyme and metres to the perfect literats of America.
Do you take it I would astonish?

Does the sunrise astonish? Does the early milkman, rattling over the stones?
Do I astonish more than they? Would you have delicate thunderbolts?

7. I launch forward, I propel the r-ideal man, the American of the future,
For I see that power is un~~fol~~ded in a great bicyclism.
What do you suppose will satisfy the Soul except to walk free upon a superior bicycle?
Imbued as they — active, receptive, often silent as they?
They do not seem to me like the old specimens.
They seem to me at last as perfect as the animals —
to that the revolving cycles truly and steadily rolled.

8. O for the paces of animals! O for the swiftness and balance of fishes and the birds!
O to be self-balanced for contingencies!
I am an ostrich, an albatross, a condor of the Andes,
I am tattooed with antelopes and birds all over,
And have distanced what is behind me for good reasons.

O to cling close to something afar off, something precarious and uproarious!
To push with resistless way, and speed off in the distance,
To speed where there is space enough and air enough at last!
I breathe the air and leave plenty after me.

9. You there, hesitant, limp in the knees, walking humbly, lamenting your sins;
Down-footed doubters, dull and excluded; you are eligible!
What have I to do with lamentation?
How is it I extract strength from the beef I eat?
I trip forth replenished with serene power on the bright ring of ride, the ensemble of the orbic frame, the great Biune.
On cycles fit for reception I start bigger and nimbler lads.
This way I am getting the stuff of more elevated republicans;
They are tanned in the face by glowing suns and blowing winds,
Their flesh has the old divine suppleness and strength.

10. Men of the rolly vantage, I salute you!
I see the approach of your numberless clubs — I see you understand yourselves and me.
Vivas to those who are weaned from walking and go the many-mileing gait!
I beat triumphal drums with my head,
I blow through all my embouchures my loudest and gayest music to you.
We slip the trammels of space and time, we level poise our glittering flight;
Inland and by the sea-coast and boundary lines, and we pass all boundary lines.
Our swift ordinances are on their way over the whole earth.

This with apologies to the Poet of Humanity and America — and so an

END.

www.ingramcontent.com/pod-product-compliance
Lightning Source LLC
Chambersburg PA
CBHW020138170426
43199CB00010B/799